THE COMIC STRIP DINOSAURS

RAAH!

WAAH!

Sally Kindberg and Tracey Turner

BLOOMSBURY

THE COMIC STRIP BOOK OF DINOSAURS

Bloomsbury Publishing, London, Berlin, New York and Sydney

First published in Great Britain in July 2012 by Bloomsbury Publishing Plc
50 Bedford Square, London, WC1B 3DP

Text copyright © Tracey Turner 2012
Illustrations © Sally Kindberg 2012

The moral rights of the author and illustrator have been asserted

A CIP catalogue record for this book is available from the British Library

ISBN 978 1 4088 1746 9

FSC
www.fsc.org
MIX
Paper from
responsible sources
FSC® C019704

Printed in Singapore by Tien Wah Press

1 3 5 7 9 10 8 6 4 2

www.bloomsbury.com

Contents

RRAAARGH!!!

1

BEFORE THE DINOSAURS

Earth, 4.6 billion years ago

Earth, 3.8 billion years ago

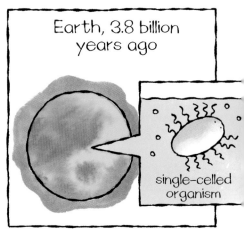

single-celled organism

Not much happened for billions of years. Then . . .

blip blop

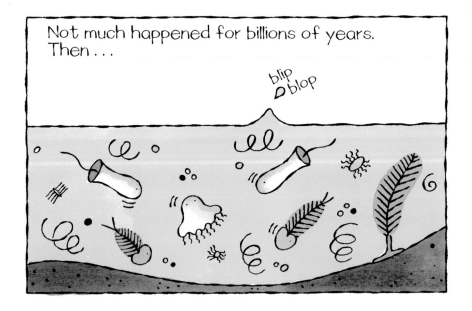

5

And then . . .

All sorts of amazing creatures turned up
(not all of these are from the same time).

7

11

HOW TO MAKE A FOSSIL

Usually, when an animal dies its body rots away over time . . .

. . . leaving nothing at all.

Sometimes, dead plants and animals can become buried in mud or sand, where they're safe from scavengers and bacteria.

A few million years later . . . The pressure of the water turns the sand into sandstone.

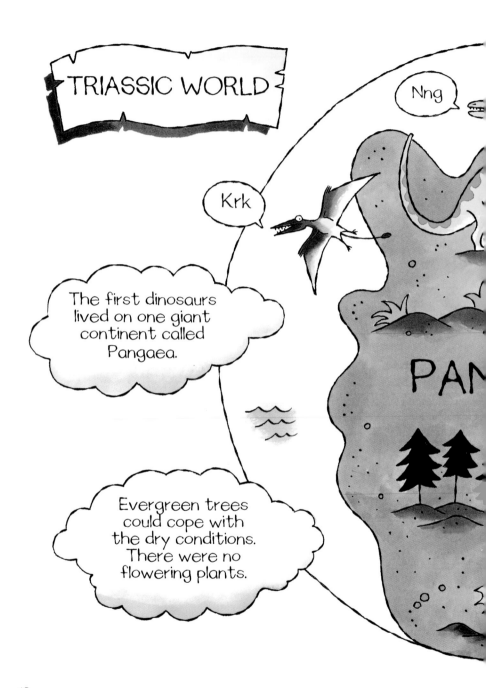

19

THE FIRST DINOSAURS

The first dinosaurs evolved from prehistoric reptiles.

Lots of reptiles were still around once dinosaurs had evolved . . .

Dinosaurs weren't the main land animals until the Jurassic.

SLURP

GNASH

We're Eoraptors – some of the earliest dinosaurs.

We look fierce and eat meat.

But we're not that big – only a metre long.

* At least, this is the most likely explanation.

23

27

JURASSIC WORLD

LAURAS[

Hnn

Pangaea split into two continents during the Jurassic.

AKK

GON

The climate was warm, but not as hot and dry as it had been during the Triassic. There weren't so many deserts but there were still no ice caps.

There were lots of palm trees and ferns, and more variety of plants.

The first birds evolved from dinosaurs.

The first true mammals appeared.

Scientists used to think Stegosaurus had an extra, bigger brain in its bum! It didn't - the brain-like lump was probably just where lots of nerves entered the animal's spinal column.

JURASSIC PREDATORS

Some scary meat-eating dinosaurs roamed the Earth in Jurassic times.

Here's our theory . . .

But none were as big as . . .

35

GIANT DINOSAUR FACTS

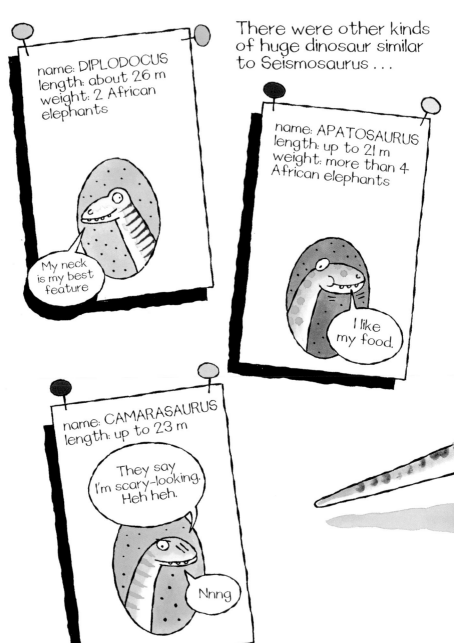

No one knows why dinosaurs like Brachiosaurus evolved to be so enormous – maybe to reach food that other creatures couldn't or to stop meat-eaters from attacking them.

But not all Jurassic dinosaurs were enormous . . .   37

41

CRETACEOUS WORLD

The continents had separated and were drifting apart.

The world was becoming cooler, though there were still no polar ice caps.

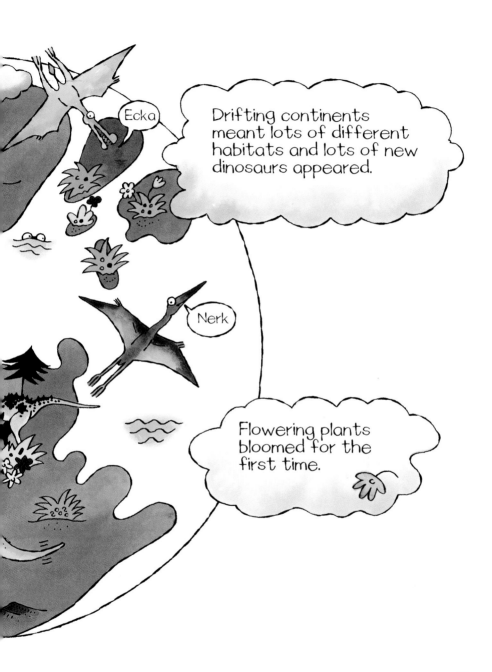

47

CRETACEOUS CRESTS

In the Cretaceous, some fancy-looking dinosaurs appeared.

Like us Maiasauras.

We had beaks . . .

and lots of teeth at the back to grind up tough plants.

I'm a Corythosaurus.

Some duck-billed dinosaurs had crests too.

Impressive, aren't they?

Sniff

Call that a crest?

Inside the hollow crests were tubes, which connected to the dinosaur's nose and throat.

We think the duck-billed dinosaurs used them to make sounds.

Nnng! Nnnng! Nnnng!

Duck-billed dinosaurs weren't the only ones
with impressive headgear . . .

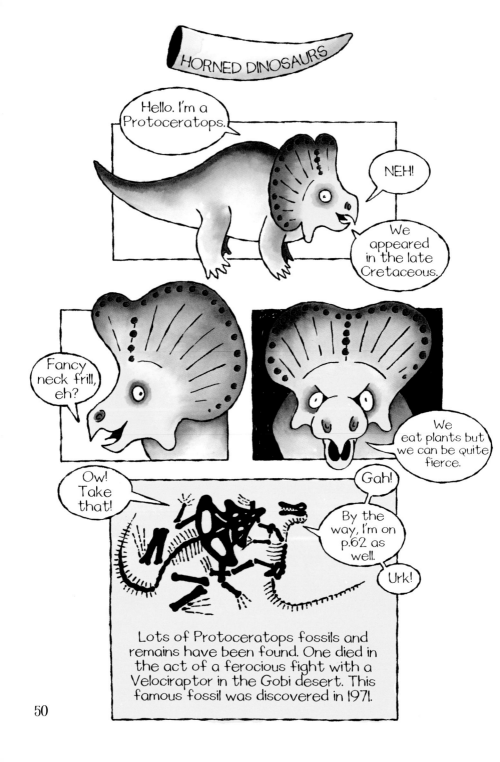

50

And some dinosaurs were
impressive in other ways . . .

HEAD-BUTTING DINOSAURS

Some Cretaceous dinosaurs had really thick skulls. They might have head-butted one another to fight off rivals. Or maybe they butted one another's bodies.

Oi! Who are you calling thick?

NUH!

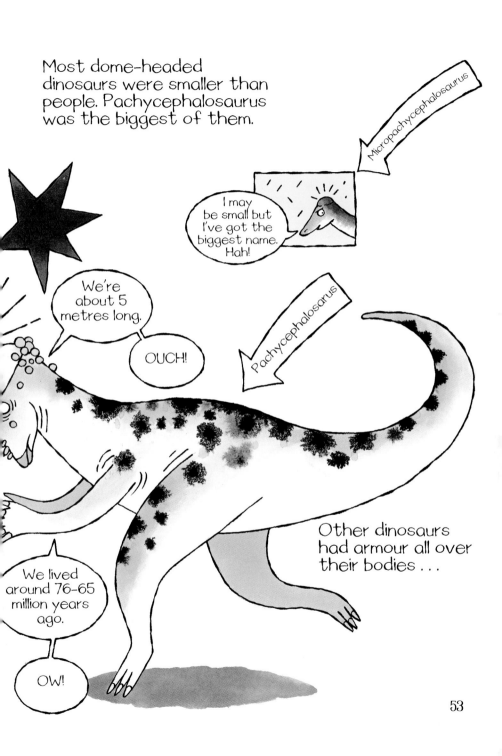

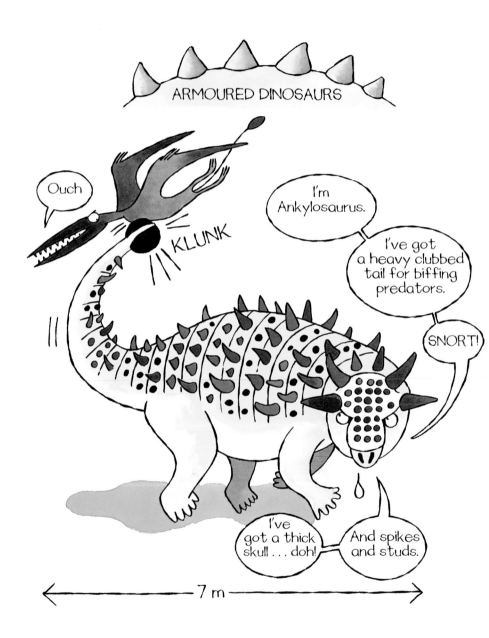

These two ate plants. But there were plenty of flesh-eaters about ...

FISH-EATERS

Another Cretaceous dinosaur has become the most famous of all . . .

TYRANNOSA

Prowling western North America 67 million years ago was a huge, ferocious flesh-eating monster . . .

Tyrannosaurus rex is so famous because 30 different skeletons have been found. The most complete is called Sue.

RF

Body
12 metres
long

T. rex looks like a predator, but some scientists argue it might have been a scavenger (because of those titchy arms). Maybe it was both. They also disagree over how fast T. rex could run. Some suggest 40 km/h, while others reckon it was half that, or even slower.

OTHER ENORMOUS FLESH-EATING MONSTERS

But smaller hunters were probably much cleverer . . .

61

RAPTORS!

Velociraptors lived in the late Cretaceous.

Look at my deadly fangs and claws!

Har har!

We're quick . . . and clever too!

Neh!

There were lots of these smaller hunters around in the Cretaceous.

Some of us, like me, a kind of Microraptor, might have been able to fly.

Wheee!

We're coming to get you.

Wokka Wokka

63

65

DINOSAUR FOOTPRINTS

During the Age of the Dinosaurs, there was a huge sea in the middle of North America.

We've found dinosaur footprints in the states of New Mexico, Colorado and Wyoming on what used to be the western shoreline.

Hundreds of dinosaur tracks have been preserved – so many that scientists have suggested it might have been a dinosaur migration route.

The most common tracks probably belong to Iguanodons or very similar dinosaurs.

Other tracks were made by ostrich-like meat-eating dinosaurs.

SCRAMBLED EGGS!

← No!

All dinosaurs laid eggs . . .
but whose is whose?

a.

The first dinosaur eggs
ever discovered, and
the largest.

b.
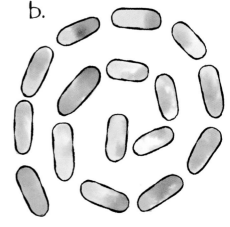

Eggs laid in spiral.

c.

Found in lots of nests
all in the same place in
Montana, USA.

d.

Eggs sometimes laid in a row.

e.

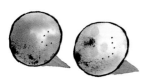

Smallest eggs
found so far.

f.

Eggs about
12 cm long.

Then, about 65 million years ago . . .

In Mexico in the 1990s, scientists discovered a massive crater left by an asteroid or a comet.

of such a huge object would create huge tsunamis hundreds of metres high.

And clouds of hot dust, which would block out the Sun and cause the Earth to cool down...

There are other (weirder) theories . . .

Caterpillars ate all the plants so there was nothing left for the plant-eaters.

munch munch

Flowering plants didn't agree with dinosaur digestion.

BURP!!

Excuse me!

The dinosaurs suffered from arthritis and tooth decay.

throb

creak

The mammals ate all the dinosaurs' eggs.

Y

The only dinosaur relatives who survived were birds!
A few other creatures made it too.

And another group of creatures survived too . . .

Over millions of years, all sorts of amazing mammals evolved from creatures called synapsids . . .

Dimetrodon

Believe it or not, we're related.

Really? How . . . lovely to meet you.

My smaller relatives survive today. But they have such disappointing teeth.

Smil

RARGH!

Whiffle

Macrauchenia

Cosy!

Early mammals ha pouches for t young. And marsupials s have then

77

EXCITING DINOSAUR FACTS

The longest dinosaur yet discovered is probably Seisr

THE FIRST DINOSAURS DISCOVERED (PROBABLY)

They were found in Sichuan, China 2,000 years ago. But they didn't know what they were...

Want to buy some dragon bones?

THE SMALLEST DINOSAUR?

This feathered dinosaur was only 25 cm long, and weighed less than 200 grammes. But it is difficult to say which is the smallest for sure, as small fossils might be those of young dinosaurs.

I'm Epidexipteryx

THE DUMBEST DINOSAURS

Based on size of brain compared to size of dino, the big plant-eaters and armoured dinosaurs like Stegosaurus were the most stupid.

Lime

Stegosaurus brain

THE EARLIEST DINOSAURS

230-million-year-old fossils were found on the island of Madagascar. Scientists have now found dinosaur-like footprints in 250-million-year-old rock - so they may have existed even earlier.

But I don't feel a day over 220 million years old.

Tracey Turner

Tracey Turner writes about lots of different
subjects, including famous writers, deadly peril,
the entire history of the Universe and, of course,
prehistoric monsters. She lives in Bath with Tom
and their son, Toby.

Sally Kindberg

Sally Kindberg is an illustrator and writer. She once went to Elf School in Iceland, has written a book about hair, sailed on a tall ship to Portugal and drawn the complete history of the world and the Universe. She likes to encourage other people to draw stuff they've never thought of drawing before, and runs workshops for them. Sally has a daughter called Emerald, and lives in London with 94 robots.

www.sallykindberg.co.uk

And for more Comic Strip History genius, don't miss ...

The Entire History of the World as it's
never been seen before. Includes the most
gripping, ghastly and slightly unexpected
things to have happened in the last several
billion years (with pictures).

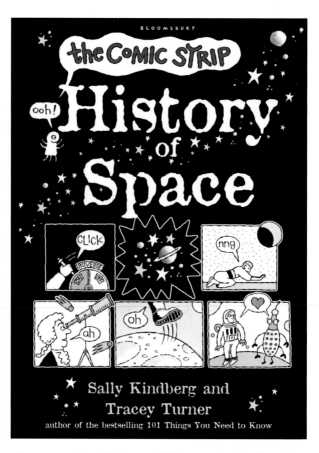

An amazing History of Space, featuring the
ENTIRE KNOWN UNIVERSE
plus some bits we're still not sure about
(with pictures).

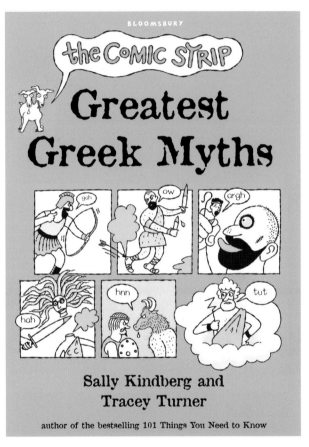

Discover the Greatest and most Gruesome
Greek Myths as they've never been told
before. From Trojans to Argonauts via the
odd Minotaur and some eye-gouging,
all the most exciting facts are revealed
(with pictures).